# We R What We 8

poetry

consumerism:
reshaping thought

by
**alonna shaw**

ISBN 978-0-9993213-0-0

FierceFriendly Press, United States
Copyright ©2017 Alonna Shaw
All Rights Reserved

This collection of aleatory poetry excerpts found material from an image.

This act of anti-poetry literally expresses how words can reshape thought.

Just change the order.

The how of what I'm doing is the what.

—Al Filreis,
Founder, Kelly Writers House,
and ModPo Convener

we are what we ate
consumerism series
ham help four las
per 1/2 cup as packaged
**nutrition facts**
serving size
**calories**
100 calories salt sodium sugar 2
craft macaroni and cheeZe
yummiest cheesiest
naturally flavored
add ground
see instructions
facts for "'as prepared" information
**total fat**

hand in hand
we were young and could run
splash knee deep in
seE water
Campbell's condensed
Paris International Exposition 1900
circle the R
registered trademark symbol
chicken noodle soup net
original flavor
smile
it's
the dinner original
per package
good news!
nine grams of protein per serving
good source of calcium
"sodium content"
enlarged to show detail
unprepared
a parenthetical…

see nutrition information
see nutrition facts

see nutrition information
see nutrition facts

we were young and could run
ge
**total fat**
a
goo
cra caro d chee

splash knee deep
chicken no
circle
original flavor
100 calo-dium sugar 2

we
enlarged
good news!
to sho-add ground
detail

Paris International Exposition 1900
100 calories salt sodium sugar 2
circle the R
good source of calcium
see nutrition information
see nutrition facts
enlarged to show detail
add ground
a parenthetical...
hand in hand
we are what we ate
**total fat**
facts for "'as prepared" information
nine grams of protein per serving
"sodium content"
per package
unprepared
good news!
original flavor
the dinner original

yummiest cheesiest
serving size
see instructions
it's
per 1/2 cup as packaged
ham help four las
splash knee deep in
Campbell's condensed
craft macaroni and cheeZe
chicken noodle soup net
we were young and could run
smile
**nutrition facts**
seE water
registered trademark symbo
**calories**
consumerism series
naturally flavored

unprepared
it's
smile
hand in hand
seE water
Paris International Exposition 1900
**total fat**
enlarged to show detail
"sodium content"
splash knee deep in
add ground
ham help four las
circle the R
see instructions
yummiest cheesiest
see nutrition information
see nutrition facts
the dinner original
registered trademark symbol
facts for "as prepared" information
a parenthetical...
consumerism series
we are what we ate
good news!

nine grams of protein per serving
good source of calcium
naturally flavored
serving size
Campbell's condensed
**nutrition facts**
craft macaroni and cheeZe
100 calories salt sodium sugar 2
per 1/2 cup as packaged
**calories**
chicken noodle soup net
per package

## ham help four las

naturally flavored
100 calories salt sodium sugar 2
original flavor
**calories**
"sodium content"
**nutritional facts**
see nutrition information
see nutrition facts
nine grams of protein per serving
per 1/2 cup as packaged
craft macaroni and cheeZe
Campbell's condensed
serving size
good source of calcium

we were young and could run
enlarged to show detail
consumerism series
registered trademark symbol
unprepared
it's
hand in hand
circle the R
we are what we ate
chicken noodle soup net
seE water
per package
Paris International Exposition 1900
add ground
smile
a parenthetical…
**total fat**
see instructions
the dinner original
splash knee deep in
good news!
yummiest cheesiest
facts for "as prepared" information

| | | |
|---|---|---|
| smile | we are what we ate | ham help four las |
| package per | | |
| 100 calories salt sodium sugar | | **nutritional facts** |
| original flavor | "sodium" | it's            re |
| nine grams of per serving | see nut format | |
| see nutrition facts | circle the R | |
| calcium of source good | per 1/2 cup as packaged | |
| a parenthetical… | ampbe condensed | bl |
| ser            **total fat** | International Exposition | |
| naturally flavored | und            d knee splash | |
| facts for "as pre | nner original | |
| yummiest cheesiest | see instructions | |
| | good news! | |

        we were young and could run

       hand in hand       consumerism series
gistered trade symbol
   raft mac-ni and eZe     **calories**


ank white
 1900     so noodle chicken

a parenthetical...
hand in hand
we are what we ate

ham help four las
facts for "as prepared" information
see instructions
we were young and could run
yummiest cheesiest
splash knee deep in
**calories**

serving size
seE water
circle the R
"sodium content"
smile

unprepared
see nutrition information see nutrition facts
the dinner original

**nutrition facts**

add ground
**total fat**
it's


enlarged to show detail
registered trademark symbol
good news!
naturally flavored
Paris International Exposition 1900

consumerism series

per package
Campbell's condensed
chicken noodle soup net
good source of calcium
original flavor
nine grams of protein per serving
100 calories salt sodium sugar 2
per 1/2 cup as packaged
craft macaroni and cheeZe

we are what we ate
hand in hand
facts for "as prepared" information
we were young and could run

a parenthetical...
it's
registered trademark symbol
circle the R

add ground
consumerism series
enlarged to show detail
**calories**

Paris International Exposition 1900
yummiest cheesiest
seE water
naturally flavored

smile
unprepared
good news!
see instructions

splash knee deep in
ham help four las

**total fat**

see nutrition instructions
see nutrition facts

"sodium content"
the dinner original

**nutrition facts**
serving size

per package
Campbell's condensed
chicken noodle soup net
good source of calcium
original flavor
nine grams of protein per serving
100 calories salt sodium sugar 2
per 1/2 cup as packaged
craft macaroni and cheeZe

consumerism series
enlarged to show detail
add ground
registered trademark symbol
yummiest cheesiest
good news!
it's
a parenthetical…

per package
Campbell's condensed
chicken noodle soup net
good source of calcium
original flavor
nine grams of protein per serving
100 calories salt sodium sugar 2
per 1/2 cup as packaged
craft macaroni and cheeZe

we were young and could run
smile
splash knee deep in
unprepared
facts for "as prepared" information

**total fat**
see nutrition information
see nutrition facts
"sodium content"
the dinner original
**nutrition facts**
serving size

hand in hand
we are what we ate
see instructions

circle the R
seE water
naturally flavored

**calories**
Paris International Exposition 1900
ham help four las

hand in hand
it's
registered trademark symbol

see instructions

good news!
a parenthetical...
facts for "as prepared" inform

yummiest cheesiest
smile
enlarged to show detail

seE water
we are what we ate
unprepared
consumerism series

splash knee deep in
we were young and could run

add ground

naturally flavored

per package
Campbell's condensed
chicken noodle soup net
good source of calcium
original flavor
nine grams of protein per serving
100 calories salt sodium sugar 2
per 1/2 cup as packaged
craft macaroni and cheeZe

**total fat**
see nutrition information see
nutrition facts
"sodium content"
the dinner original
**nutrition facts**
serving size

**calories**
Paris International Exposition
1900
ham help four las

we are what we ate

enlarged to show detail
we were young and could run
unprepared
hand in hand

seE water
it's
facts for "as prepared" information
splash knee deep in

good news!
see instructions
a parenthetical…
yummiest cheesiest


circle the R
registered trademark symbol
smile

per package
Campbell's condensed
chicken noodle soup net
good source of calcium
original flavor
nine grams of protein per serving
100 calories salt sodium sugar 2
per 1 /2 cup as packaged
craft macaroni and cheeZe

**total fat**
see nutrition information
see nutrition facts
"sodium content"
the dinner original
**nutrition facts**
serving size

**calories**
Paris International Exposition 1900
ham help four las

naturally flavored

add ground
consumerism

we are what we ate    enlarged ~~to~~ show detail       we were young
         unprepared                    hand in hand

seE water              it's                             facts for "as
splash knee deep in    good news!
         see instructions       smile


a parenthetical…      yummiest cheesiest       circle   the
       register~~ed~~ trademark symbol
                              **total fat**

and could run

prepared" information


R

naturally flavored
add ground
consumerism series

per package
Campbell's condensed
chicken noodle soup net
good source of calcium
original flavor
nine grams of protein per serving
100 calories salt sodium sugar 2
per 1/2 cup as packaged
craft macaroni and cheeZe



see nutrition information
see nutrition facts
"sodium content"
the dinner original
nutrition facts
serving size

calories
Paris International Exposition 1900
ham help four las

                it's
                good news!
                hand in hand

regist~~ered~~ trademark symbol          see instructions
a parenthetical...                      facts for "as prepared
enlarged ~~to~~ show detail               seE water

                yummiest cheesiest
                circle the R
                we were young and could run

**total fat**                                       smile
we are what we ate                    unprepared
splash knee deep in                   (blank)

" information

naturally flavored
add ground
consumerism series

per package
Campbell's condensed
chicken noodle soup net
good source of calcium
original flavor
nine grams of protein per serving
100 calories salt sodium sugar 2
per 1/2 cup as packaged
craft macaroni and cheeZe

see nutrition information
see nutrition facts
"sodium content"
the dinner original
**nutrition facts**
serving size

**calories**
Paris International Exposition 1900
ham help four las

   it's
        seE water
                we were young and could run
                      smile
                              splash knee deep in

        facts for "as prepared" information
                **total fat**
                        good news!

enlarged ~~to~~ show detail
        circle the R
                a parenthetical...

                        unprepared

naturally flavored
add ground
consumerism series

per package
Campbell's condensed
chicken noodle soup net
good source of calcium
original flavor
nine grams of protein per serving
100 calories salt sodium sugar 2
per 1/2 cup as packaged

craft macaroni and cheeZe

registered trademark symbol
see instructions

see nutrition information
see nutrition facts
"sodium content"
the dinner original
**nutrition facts**
serving size

**calories**
Paris International Exposition 1900
ham help four las
yummiest cheesiest

it's
       seE water
              we were young and could run
                     smile
                            splash knee deep in

       facts for "as prepared" information
            **total fat**
                    good news!

enlarged ~~to~~ show detail
      circle the R
             a parenthetical…


                        unprepared

splash

        knee

                deep

                        in

**total fat**
    unprepared

add ground
consumeris
facts for "as p
larged ~~to~~ show
per package
Campbell's con
chicken noodle
good source of
original flavor
nine grams
100 calories
per 1/2 cup a
craft macaro
register~~ed~~ t
see instruct
see nutriti
see nutriti
"sodium
the dinn
**nutrition**
serving s
**calories**
Paris Int
ham he

**total fat**
    unprepared

naturally flavored
add ground
consumerism series
facts for "as prepared" information
enlarged ~~to~~ show detail
per package
Campbell's condensed
chicken noodle soup net
good source of calcium
original flavor
nine grams of protein per serving
100 calories salt sodium sugar 2
per 1/2 cup as packaged
craft macaroni and cheeZe
registe~~red~~ trademark symbol
see instructs
see nutrition information
see nutrition facts
"sodium content"
the dinner original
**nutrition facts**
serving size
**calories**
Paris International Exposition 1900
ham help four las
yummiest cheesiest

        patent pending
**total fat**
        GLAD
              unprepared

**total fat**
3 cnb unprepared
smile
      good
            water

**total fat**
unprepared
smile
ate we what are we
good news!

naturally flavo
add ground
consumerism
facts for "as p
arged ~~to~~ sho
per package
Campbell
chicken
good
or

**total fat**     unprepared
smile   ate we what are we
(double crossed)

s'ti
smile
circle we are what we ate
good news!
we were young and could run
retaw ees
a parenthetical...

smile it's

good news!

seE water

circle we are what we ate

we were young and could run

a parenthetical...

craft

add grouna
facts for "as prepared" information      heeZe
enlarged to
           cheesiest
100                                      ham help four las
good sourc caum          per serving     's condensed
per packa
         **calories**      serving size

OR


Original flavor

ham help four las's condensed heeZe facts for "as prepared" infor 100 good sourc **calories** pe packa ca-um er serving

original flavor




mation craft add grouna enlarged cheesiest condensed serving size

good ne ate coul-nng original dinner the **nutrition** eZe a

                        Consumerism series
                        see instructions
                        see nutrition information
                        see nutrition facts
                        enlarged t~~o~~ show detail
                        register~~ed~~ trade symbol
                        Paris Int Exp 00
                        per packag

chicken noodle soup net
good source of calcium

smile ce the R
good ne
what ate
n coul ug were we
hand

al flavor
"sodium content" serving per protein of grams nine
craft macaroni and cheeZe
**facts nutritional** the dinner original
per 1/2 cur as packaged
naturally flavored add gr serv ng size

Consumerism series
see instructions
see nutrition information
see nutrition facts
enlarged to show detail
registered trade symbol
Paris Int Exp 00
per packag

good news!
ervi nprepared facts for "as pare" atio

ham
a pare
salt sodium sugar
siest dem we we

serving unprepared facts for "as prepared" information
good news!

**nutrition facts**
it's
a parenthetical...

see instructions

    hand in hand

**total fat**

      ham help four las

smile

      circle the R

we are what we ate

      we were young and could run

enlarged ~~to~~ show detail

      splash knee deep in

facts for "as prepared" information

    see nutrition information
    see nutrition facts

    consumerism series
  Paris International Exposition     1900

unprepared
register~~ed~~ trademark symbol

yummiest seE water original good news 100 calories salt s-um ackage rally v **calo** size-ing sodium and cheeZe dinner original vor nine gra-of pr serving kaged

show your workspace
show your work

show your tools

what is left without the container
two forms
both unclear
sharing the same ground
not far apart
different approaches
word
order

8

we are what we ate

## Notes.

I grew up making toys out of what I encountered. My mind leaping from pages gripping words to pave a path among porcupines and lilac trees.

The first time I heard the expression *sweep the kitchen* occurred when I was ordering pizza while visiting my dad in West Monroe, Louisiana. In this context, it meant "use everything you have on hand."

The next time I heard someone use this expression was on a Sunday afternoon in Tokyo, Japan. My roommate and I, as models, were used to being the ones compelling consumers to consume. We were hungry and had little in our refrigerator to consume. She suggested we sweep the kitchen. Instant ramen noodles with some odds-n-ends of wilted vegetables and unagi (freshwater eel) on the side. The lack of veggie crunch no longer a problem in their adjusted form as soup.

I've since modified the expression to mean "use anything you have at hand." I've appropriated a simple pizza order and applied it to my art and writing technique as *use what you have*.

By applying constraints to my sweep-the-kitchen technique, these imposed rules create discovery possibilities.

> Recipe:
> Select only three main ingredients.
> Set aside a couple extra as seasoning options.

For this collection of found poems, I selected three main ingredients:

> Printed words from an image I created; scissors; and a plastic bowl.
> My metaphorical herbs enhancing the main ingredients were a black cork mat and a pencil.

It all bubbled up together. My procedures whittled down the paper strip count. A temporary display on the black cork mat captured by an iPhone 7 showed the evolving voice and made it possible to share in text and image.

# On this book.

"How we say" is in what we choose to consume orally, aurally, viscerally, spiritually, and physically. I asked myself, "With what moments do we fill our photo frames and the dusty spaces too inconvenient to rid of past accumulation? How do we pass down what we are?"

My uncreative assembling of lines grew out of a creative act where I juxtaposed what we consume with photo frames on a prominent place of display, the family mantle. A day of photographing from many perspectives returned me to the original test shot where my dust cloth lingered between the frames. My art recipe instructed the procedure. You witness the text in this book. The photos remain as an annotated aleatory workbook.

I found my poem by free-form excerpting from my source photo and then let randomness influence line remixing. The image provided the majority of the found language, supplemented by bits of writing, like describing the atmosphere of the two children in the photo frame. Poems were transcribed in order of discovery.

Punctuation and bolding were transferred from package to the poem source text. Substitution of actual parenthesis as a description: "a parenthetical." I took the creative nostalgic liberty to convey tone by capitalizing the *z* in "cheeZe" and changing the brand name Kraft™ to reflect the craft of creating. Intentional misspelling of sea as "seE" invites the reader to participate.

The way the paper strips fell when dumped from the plastic Glad™ tub dictated harvesting order plus spacing and flow. How the paper strips fell determined stanza breaks, columns, or other forms. Columns permitted reading both horizontally and vertically.

I noticed line counts, syllables, enjambment, and read them out loud. Pieces of words, blank spaces, and directions became clues to follow on this synaptic exploration where randomness permitted unprotected insight. Perhaps a closer look would open unprocessed thinking? But I knew processing must be delayed as long as possible.

"Move on to the next shuffle" became my mantra. I'd remind myself, just read for sound, structure, beats, pedagogy examples, etc.—no rearranging—and move on to the next shuffle. Restrain from contriving meaning. Permit randomness.

When I succumbed to temptation by noting syllable counts on the strips and striking through "to" and "ed" to find meaning within the words, I removed my glasses as an unplanned constraint, impeding further temptation of word manipulation. Static cling caused pieces to stick to the plastic Glad™ container and get overlooked. I embraced this mistake as random selection. The monotony of the text inspired separating lines into columns by fact- vs. emotion-based content. I tried to maintain personal distance from the content.

Unusual transcriptions include formatting variations due to this book's page size being smaller than the original workbook. "Double crossed" (p. 33) reflects how the strips appeared. Upside down strips translate as spelling backwards (p. 34). Eventually, I whittled down the project by rejecting one column dense with marketing text to see what remained.

Variations from the original workbook form: some poems have been spread across two pages to accommodate this book's smaller page dimensions (pp. 4/5, 6/7, 8/9, 10/11, 12/13, 14/15, 18/19, 20/21, 22/23, 24/25, 36/37, 42/43). Modifications on page 17 include "information" has been shortened to "inform" and line wrapping treatment aligns with the outside edge of the preceding line fragment's end "see nutrition information see nutrition facts" and "1900."

Pages 44-47 stray from the paper strip content as a kind of reflective process summary.

I wondered: would the reader's nostalgia stir together current life constraints, enlivening these disparate lines?

## On my Consumerism Series.

When family values became processed slogans, we lost personal validation, generating consumers instead of citizens. Consuming equals validation. A hopeless equation.

My Consumerism Series consists of poems, images, video poetry, a workbook, an annotated workbook, and this book.

What hole in our society's emotional makeup creates empty calories?

# Acknowledgments.

My hope is that online education will determine a connected future where we don't need to be divided by race, color, age, gender, religion, or anything else, if learning motives us. A kind heart and an open mind supply the prerequisites. Massive Open Online Courses (MOOCs) rocked my world. The University of Pennsylvania's Modern Poetry course known as ModPo and the people within it saved me. From what? Suffice it to say life is hard—

> Allow the swerves, the shattered dreams, the sleepless nights, and move on. Follow what is doable, what exists. Splinters can be more memorable than the wood from which they strayed. I am so thankful to be part of the ModPo community.

My deep appreciation goes to poet Joseph Massey, who acted as editor for this experimental work. Whose kind support, extensive experience grounded in form and randomness, and insightful feedback bolstered my confidence. Any errors are my own.

Thank you always to my husband who reminds me daily he believes in me and my creative path. That my swing dancing Pony Express rider's mind and spirit have something to say.

Time to share it.


More at alonnashaw.com

*Cover and interior design by author.*
*Main digital source image created and captured in color, February 2016 by Alonna Shaw (beach image contained within of two children used with permission of Robertstock/ClassicStock).*

www.ingramcontent.com/pod-product-compliance
Lightning Source LLC
Chambersburg PA
CBHW061343040426
42444CB00011B/3061